Letters from the singularity

poems

Josie Di Sciascio-Andrews

Letters from the singularity

by

Josie Di Sciascio-Andrews

Published by: In Our Words Inc./www.inourwords.ca

Cover image: © liyavihola Shutterstock.com

Book design: Shirley Aguinaldo

Library and Archives Canada Cataloguing in Publication

Di Sciascio-Andrews, Josie, 1955-, author
Letters from the singularity : poems / Josie Di Sciascio-Andrews.

ISBN 978-1-926926-50-6 (pbk.)

I. Title.

PS8607.I73L48 2015 C811›.6 C2015-901289-9

For my mother: my guiding light

Prologue

"You can check out any time you want,
but you can never leave."

'Hotel California,' The Eagles

Table of contents

On the Title... 6
Awakening in the Night 8
Event Horizon 12
Flowers in Blue Vase 13
In Nonna's House 15
Portal 17
Leaving 20
Woman Sitting at Bus Stop 21
No Man's Land 22
Geraniums on a Patio in Positano 23
The Red Accordion 25
Blue Evening 28
The Wild Things 29
Moon Birth 31
"One Day You Will Understand Me," My Father Said. 33
Earwig 35
Poetic Alchemy 37
Premonition 38
Nocturne 41
The Hidden City 43
Evolution 46
Thrift Shop 47
Magical Woods 48
A Jar of Fireflies 50
Picking Lilacs 52
Out of Nothing 53
Of Love and Writing 55
Rain 57

Life Rounded Up 59
The Harbour 60
The Surface of Things 61
Raison D'etre 62
Your Return 63
Summer Evening 64
Glendella House 66
Contemplation on a Miniature Jade Fountain in a Chinese Restaurant 68
Immigrants Fishing on the Oakville Pier 70
Murdered Gods 72
Love's Treasure 74
Dangerous Reflection 76
Emerald City 77
A Lesson of Pieces 78
Christmas Memories 80
Creation 82
The Aloe Plant on my Mother's Windowsill 84
Summer Dreams 86
Driving Home From Toronto on the QEW 87
Saturday Night in Suburbia 88
War on the Planet 89
Moonless Dark 90
Broken Glass 91
Victoria Day Fireworks 92
Trajectory 94
My Human Identity 96
A Poem from my Laundry Room 97
Fall in Our Town 99
Weathervane 100
Elements 102

On the title...

Since time immemorial, humans have been writing about spiritual journeys of the soul to the underworld. In various epochs and cultures, the myth has had variations, but as Jungian psychology illustrates, the archetypes always revolve around a consistent, collective unconscious human theme. Always, there is a 'spiritual falling' to a point where reality ceases to cohere. All previously held visions and certainties begin to fail. The soul is forced to accept incongruity, paradox and helplessness. It is at this point of smallness in the face of adversity, when life throws us unexpected curves and places snags in the fabric of our reality. It is here that we are forced to let go and give in to the larger forces of what we can only call divinity, an all-encompassing consciousness or nature. In *The Red Book*, Carl Jung scried mystical visions and mandalas from the depths of his own psychosis. The leitmotifs are quintessential in their similarity to St. John of the Cross' *Dark Nights of the Soul*, Jesus' fall from grace in his temptations in the desert and Dante's journey through Hell in *The Divine Comedy*.

In Einstein's Theory of Relativity, 'singularities' are snags in space-time. They are infinite points inside black holes, regions from which nothing, not even light can escape. A 'singularity,' a point in time that goes on to infinity, where reality as we know, ceases and all scientific formulas and rules break down. James Hillman writes that "when all is stripped away and life is turned upside down, the ground drops out from under us" (Hillman 43) and all the knowledge and experience we had accumulated in our lives up to that point, fail. What I love about the concept of the 'singularity' is that it is a mythic passage of the soul.

Due to life's unexpected tragedies, we fall from grace into the frightening vortex of the underworld, where all laws and rules break down, and where, indeed, there is no certainty of coming out alive: poetry the only saving grace. In the journey through the darkest abyss, classical Roman poet Virgil, guides

Dante with his words to make sense of the senseless. Poetry, then becomes the guiding light: the mind's synthesis of the singularity's incoherence. Poetry becomes the funnel back to light. Words, letters: stepping stones, guiding us back to wholeness from disintegration.

Josie

Awakening in the night

this is the hour
that gnaws like a premonition
of all that threatens
to tether the thin veil
between reality and dream

the angst ridden moment
assailing in the night
when you awaken startled
to discover how things have changed

while seamlessly the earth
rotates blue blood
towards the sun

and vapor eases darkness
into dawn... a certain clarity

of thought reminds you that everything
is spinning away from its own birth

and that the shadows of concrete things
dilute like ghosts, but energy is never lost

it goes somewhere... perhaps it re-embodies

it all makes you think of Hinduism,
of Christian Heavens, of Einstein's theory of mc^2

as moonlight splinters cool paths
from rooftops to brambled fields of milkweed

I don't know if it's panic or existential angst
this fear of change... of loss... of knowing
our own propulsion towards separation

this continuous falling out of Eden

the universe expanding from its zero point
at exponential velocities

while we draw back the faces, places
and meanings we construed like rails
in order to hang on... survive... while all around
us and within, an invisible hum
of electrons eternally spins perfect gyres
unto their incohesion

we glimpse the losses in increments:
a death here... a madness there... loves
shredded by the obtuseness of the stupid

philosophies, paintings and great myths
remain whispering of permanence

the yin and yang of things revolving
endlessly in its own ellipse

while night hushes the strife of sunlight
and weary, we rest our heads on pillows

like children hoping to return
to some benevolent era
when we were loved

hush little baby... you have grown up
your aging hands gnarl like thistles
in winter wind

the moon is a bone
predicting your future

she neither cries nor smiles at you,
though you trace a humanness
to her face

she is your mother
cold and unreachable... she recedes
then grows again, while you slowly die
she lives on forever

this is the startling dream
that holds the moon
and your corpse in the grave
all at once

love too... and the light... it all moves you
to long backwards for what was so beautiful
once... what seemed like an eternal moment

that essence you captured in stills
of memory and forward for what will become
of you... your children

and suddenly you remember a crypt
in the catacombs of a basilica
you visited when you were young

the marble stone over a Pope's body buried
there, had sent shivers up your spine

now, you feel the stone in you
inching its way from your fingertips
into your arms, like vines
of frostbite... invisible roots

insinuating their metaphors
of nerves and veins
into your flesh... growing torsos... branches

you are the tree... the soil... the stone

although you imagined you were free,
you haven't moved

you are the landscape
the night in you as you awaken

and your windows are your eyes
panning out from your house
or anywhere, like a face

looking for itself in the mirror... in the dark

Event horizon

The music must have kept on playing
As we were riding into sunsets.
Like a soundtrack
Choreographed for an epic
Film, when abruptly,
The credits mark
The end, decreting
Deeds and names.
No one noticed
The exact time
We fell off the edge.
An event that could have
Taken place long before
Anyone observed us
Riding off the rim
Of their lens' view.
In that moment,
Crows hitched to summer dusk
Would remain iconically
Burned in someone's retina.
Static dark wings
In perennial flight
Through sienna-hued canyons.
Beyond that frame,
Unseen, the slip of tire
Or foot would pull our body's mass
Into the gravity of slope.
Any momentary contortion
Of pain would go unrecorded.
So too the havoc wrought
By impact on the solidity
Of our previously held form
To particles the likes
Of an imploding sun.

Flowers in blue vase

this blue clay vase
is rough to the touch

beneath my fingertips
the leaves are velvet tongues

still life of zinnias
daffodils and marigolds
arrange the view
on blue linen tablecloth

outside
behind the window pane
dreamscapes glisten

the earth bequests
beyond the cultivated fields
to chance our way
through groves of thickest darkness

see the empty barn
its dark blind eye

see the fields of nettles
bloodying the purple hills,
crowning them with silver clouds

between these blooms
and that far away light
the years ripple

back to the centre
pieces on another table

in another time

of another place
we once called home

In nonna's house

these are the roses
I picked in nonna's garden

these are the peaches

here is the bottle
I filled in her wine cellar

here is the carafe of olive oil

scattered on the blue tablecloth
are the books I have read

half a dozen spilled fruits

sunlight is splashing
on a framed purple sea
hanging on a yellow wall

beyond this view
a dog sleeps in the corner
ear twitching at a fly

the tap is leaking

summer breeze fills the curtain
with cicadas' circular echoes

I am but a point in space
standing
in concentric circles of memory

all those places
all those loved ones

alive
at the centre
of this still life

Portal

I awaken to the sound of wind rushing north from the lake
reiterating its cries of urgency through my slightly open
window

across the morning roads I can hear it dragging its' guttural
echoes

hushing to a hissing sibilance in the tangle of winter trees

ransacking the powdering of newly fallen snow from pine
branches,
obliged to bow to its relentless force like the frosted paws
of some benevolent animals fanning the entrance of my
musings
into the enchanted wonder of the world

snow has fallen onto the snowy path

I can see it blowing from the thatched roof across the yard

pulling my thoughts to the memory of a period armoire
filled with coats and furs

something about hiding out from war, a secret passageway
from the safety of an upstairs study into the wilderness

at once I understand C.S. Lewis conceiving Narnia

and below the snow-covered blue spruce on my lawn
a quintessential squirrel the colour of bark
darts across the frozen grass to its refuge

invisible to my naked eye, evil and goodness

lurk, rife to manifest in characters yet to be known

inside a castle's four walls an ice queen
with a frozen heart
is dreaming dystopian futures

infinite universes of infinite suns
implode then coalesce
into forever new chess boards of destinies
... and in the deserts good lions
are struggling to survive
the scourge of greed and science

half men like sphinx, like centaurs
alone in their lofts are plugging in
their human selves to technological devices,

half animal with gods and myths demoted

heaven and hell mere remnants
of archaic imaginings, guarded
by the three pronged head
of profit, taser and gun

Narnia is here

I can see it vividly this morning
like those images that pop up into relief from a sea
of dots when you've been staring at them for a while

outside my window it re-emerges
with its flurries and light posts

beckoning with its boughs of fir pointing up and out
to the pale peripheries
of this house, this street

the world fading to invisible atoms
of light and darkness

taking on the human physiognomies
of good kings and despots

with their respective armies
of horses and rooks

cast to refashion the fate of our time
with the same old rhetoric
in new words and new clothes

Leaving

We are so much like the trees.

We mistake their stasis for imprisonment.
Our mobility for freedom.

But we too are deeply rooted.
Bound in place.

Conglomerates of electrons.
Atoms spinning ghost-like
Within the predetermined orbits
Of our hearts' metaphysics.

On the doors of my house
There are no metal bars.

Unlike the trees, I escape daily
Though thousands of years
Of evolution keep me here.

Anthropology. Brain wiring.
Maternal instinct.

It all makes me think of a chunk of tree
I saw once. Trapped like flesh
Through a chain-link fence.

The tree itself, cut down.

No longer there. Just this remnant
Torso of itself forever caught
Growing towards sunlight.

Escaping through steel.
Imagining it could.

Woman sitting at bus stop

I saw her sitting
On a bench
At Third Line and Lakeshore.
Hair white as a scarecrow.
That's when it hit
Like cold wind.
Autumn leaves, snow flakes
Falling upon her
In the midst of spring.
Her vacant eyes transfixed
On faraway clock towers.
Hands clasping a purse
Of memories. Better days
Ticking on her wrist watch
Reflecting clouds
At the speed of time.
I saw her sitting silently,
Still as a statue.
Her life played out
From a to z.
That's when it hit
Like a celluloid dream.
Life fast forwarded.
Rewound.
She could be me.
And soon
She would be gone.

No man's land

(selected by Priscilla Uppal as one of the top three poems of the Canada Literary Review's Summer Sports Poetry Competition)

There is a certain comfort in the symmetry
Of striking pressurized air
Of optic yellow felt
As it is precisely loosed
From the left hand's grip,
While with well thought out,
Taut-weaved racket precision,
A backhanded right one smashes it across the court
A world over the net at centre
Stretching its equator to the tentative,
Invisible dragons lurking in the sidelines.
Adrenaline primes you into that zone
Of brain-body synchrony
Where you anticipate all angles
Of your opponent's rebuttals.
Simultaneously you shadow
Her moves as you rally, lunge
Your weight diagonally through air
Onto the gravity of rubberized concrete
To block all coups
Re-entering the dharma
Of a frantic little Dutch boy,
Should any hint of loss overtake
You. Your country.
One fault, like one drop of ocean
Beginning to stream through some tiny crack
In the solid wall of your well rehearsed,
Calculated resistance.

Geraniums on a patio in positano

(inspired by a painting by Canadian artist Geri Puley)

What is it about the colour red
That draws me in?

Like blood calling blood,

As if the rest did not exist:
The softest hues of dovetail grey
Blurring into white cloud and rock.

Pale blue skies dripping like tears.
Washing over the muted fibers
Of verdigris landscapes.

Sadness seeping deeper
In the growing emptiness
Of time slipping past.

Red instead rekindles
The eye's gaze
To flirt with the sun.

Blushes the cheeks
Of ripening fruit

In a country
I could fall in love with,
For its joyful feast of summer.
Where geranium petals
Cascade from balconies.

Bloom red like the hearts
Of women sitting
Behind old glass panes

Stoking hope like embers
To outlive the fog's paleness.

The red accordion

(shortlisted for Descant's Winston Collins Best Canadian poem prize)

By ear, at five
My father
Learned to play
An instrument too big
For tiny shoulders to endure.
On slow, hot afternoons
After a day of harvest,
Zio Domenico offered him wine,
Secrets of manhood, cigarettes.
Strapped an accordion
To his tender arms
Then taught his little fingers to seek
Out harmonic nuances
On a pearly keyboard to the right,
While cohering rhythm from the randomness
Of small, black buttons to the left.
Two ventricles
Bellowing in and out the sound
Waves of a universe expanding
From a silken, fanned out lung
Opening wide the landscape of a life,
Inevitably returning
To the corpus callosum of itself,
Collapsing beauty shut.
Like a butterfly with pleated paper wings
My father mastered syncopated rhapsodies
Molding heart to calculated sequences.
Keeping tempo
In the gaps.
Like heart beats.

Time in one hand,
Space in the other.
A tiny God
Juggling spheres.
I always remember him middle-aged
Sitting on the basement couch
Of the Oakville bungalow
He bought for us in 1970.
I still see him with a glass
Of whisky or home-made wine
Before a winter night
Shift at the refinery, teary-eyed
And nostalgic, playing old tunes
On a second-hand accordion.
I remember how it bothered him
Not to be able to reach a certain note
Because of a missing key.
He had his eye on a new, red one
That he'd seen in a music shop window
In Clarkson—was planning to buy it
After the last mortgage payment
Of what was to become
His last spring.
On the broken accordion
The quality of sound was good regardless.
How like my father to make good
Of the worst or the mediocre,
His fingers harmonizing joy
For us in allegro, andante,
Improvising the frenzied flights
Of old world soundscapes
Waltzes and tangos. Mazurkas.
Inevitably entering into the segues of silence.
The long, slow notes of a loveless winter.
And then briefly, the joyful reprieve
Of a ripresa stitching back

The sweetness of a singable refrain
From some top-forty radio hit
Like Tie a Yellow Ribbon
'Round the Old Oak Tree.
A heart zigzagging spasmodic
Sound right to the end.
Like a blood song.
A song beginning.
A song ending.
With so much urgent striving in between.

Blue evening

tonight
the lake is a blue daiquiri

my heart a raw wound
waiting to be assuaged
by wind and waves

as if they could
cauterize the hollow
blood inlets
of my unrequited longing

Buddha, Jesus,
you
walking on water
at last

stretching out your hand
to save me

The wild things

Oh how the wild things grow!
Slithering tortuous and strong in the moonlight

Suckling lymph with their tentacled roots
From the deep darkness of the moist earth.

Strong are the stalks
Of their snake like torsos.
The hairy spikes of their thistle spines.

It is so hard to pick them.

So much pain to endure
For just one precious, purple bloom.

Flowers of blood.

Cynical beauties.

Late bloomers
Adapted to self-protect.

Twice bitten lovers
With malleable hearts.

I have seen the wild things grow.
Their shadows looming tall in the night.

Multiplying of their own volition
In places beyond my reach.

How many times have I cut them down
Only to find them lush and thriving

Past my window in the morning?

I am getting used to their ever growing presence.

Tonight I can look beyond them
And still see the moon.

Tomorrow, like everything else,
I too will be of them.

Moon birth

she has seen the black edge of night
birthing a blood orange moon
lighting up the sky with misty glow

magical, dark water woman
cradling a fair-headed child

it was the face of love
she saw

the man in the moon

trailing flickering flames of memories
across dark waves

orange
red
yolk like a sun, moon

emerging out of somber depths

the world's face glowed
as if for the first time,
beyond all dreams,
bursting illusions
with unexpected moon birth

like the night her children came
and the unknown took shape
beyond her will

blood alchemy of newborn skin, eyes, lips

celestial bodies' perfect form

emerging out of water
out of darkness

"One day you will understand me," my father said.

Inside the whale
You wait for me

With your ancient wine,
Your smoldering candle.

Ageless

You sit in the dark
Corner of an epiglottis.

Dead. Yet undead.
Suspended in memory.

I have drowned.

Around my neck
A rope of heavy stones
Has snuffed out
All illusion.

Scourged
I have arrived
At your small altar
Of sacrifice.

Your shoulders are bent father.

In your eyes burns a humble wisdom
Of the world that fails.

The ominous world
of blind cats and lame foxes.

All false fire eaters.

The ocean's gaping mouth,
Maw of all things,
Like time
Has taken us.

I am here to drink
Of your cup.

Your eyes are tiny points
Of light guiding me back
From the cave
Of all unraveling.

Earwig

You hatched from your mottled egg
Glossy black, like a coffee bean.

Dexterous and slim, you unhinged
A crooked quickness from calamity
Into the fissures of furniture
And ill-fitting floor trim.

Once in horror, I watched you slide
From the plastic holes
Of an old telephone receiver.

Pincers mongering old wives tales.

Insinuating dread into ear canals,
Membrane and sinew. Entering
The sacristy of brain tissue
To clip away at reason. Bleeding me.

Curious, I searched the science
Of your claws' evolutionary purpose,
Discovering their lack of sinister motives:
Just sensual arms for gripping mates.

It made me think of the silhouette of a man
I saw once through a pub's window.

Arms gesticulating explanations
To the still shadow of a woman
Sitting across from him.

In the light, behind the frosted glass
His arms moved like that.

Hands stiff like meat hooks.

One night while I sleep,
You will exit
From your refuge of wall and floor board
To clank your tiny armored shell
Onto the polished wood of my night table.

You will dare your way upon my pillow
Dangling from hair to skin
Tearing me from dreams

With the sudden tickle
Of everything I have been averting

As you knock unexpectedly

From the invisible apertures
Of my seemingly safe house.

Poetic alchemy

I spin golden words from my world of straw.
I extrapolate wonder from the commonplace.

The centre is anywhere I am.

For there is no other place
No other happiness
Other than the piece of sky
I expand with my yearning.

My eyes create reality
With the poetic palette of blood hues:
The deep reds, the melancholy blues.

I strike a match on stone
And memory ignites it to diamond.

I immortalize people and places
I have loved.

The real world pales
While within me,

The universe explodes
With the infinite

Colours of creation.

Premonition

The wind is coming
my darling.

The gusts will arrive
unexpectedly

Like those express trains
from exotic places,

rushing out of dark tunnels,

then braking hastily
with premonitions
of love and happiness.

The wind is coming
my love.

It will blow dust,
newspaper pages

in the odd, oblique light
of unsettling dreams,

cutting geometrical shadows
against the glow
of bare city streets.

It will toss
in the mad dance
of branches

bending signs
and certainties.

With winter's skeletal fingers
it will rap its' ghostly bones
at our windowpanes

startling us
from the trance of sleep.

It will bend the oleander
bloom, disperse its scent
of pungent newness,

dishevel ivy's long tendrils
from wrought-iron balconies.

The wind is coming
my darling.

You will hear its growing clap
echoing

in the mad frenzy
of chimes.

It will tame the anger

Soften the spunk
of new skin's turgor.

Release illusions.

Undo all reason,
making of hope
a weary promise.

It will toss belief
into a fitful sleep
urging us to surrender

to the heavy quilt
of mystery

strewn like debris
of time
across our hearts

asking us only in return
for our quiescence.

Nocturne

Against blue darkness
tall pines
etch ominous crystals
in the cave of night.
Their inverted roots
burrowing deep shadows
in vast emptiness.
North star, a pin
firm in its place
holds up the night
like a circus tent
above our town.
I stand
on a velvet fold
of karma.
All unuttered thoughts
bouncing back
to their own source
of gravity.
Such agile gymnasts
elastic on their trampolines.
Trapeze artists skimming tightropes.
Elephants, tigers
braving hoops of deathly flames.
Parades of human talent,
Beauties, frightening beasts
Flaunting their tamed, glittered ferocities.
Each gift. Each oddity
of the whole gaudy world
dangling from ropes
in mid-air
as an audience forever gasps
at the expected drum roll.

We, the acrobats
with our telltale garb.
Our own bejeweled limbs flailing.
Leaping towards other hands.
Blindly seeking. Grasping
at solid objects
in the ever growing possibility
of falling
without nets.

The hidden city

Zooming in
up close,
the postcard memory
of a place
disappears.
With magnification
the edges fade,
as asphalt, brick and skin
expose their microscopic
infinities.
Panning out,
everything reverts
back to incognito delineations
of grey, concrete architecture.
The city floats
on a flat line of perception.
High and low rises accrue
solidity like stalagmites.
Below their cellared caves,
in humid undergrounds,
commuters inch their way
through revolving doors,
down metal escalators
to the netherworld
of subway tunnels.
Depending on who we are
or where we stand, human
accampments are mutable.
Like everything else we see
with the naked eye,
they unfold, beyond a myriad buildings
and facades, their many hidden secrets.
Because like a love affair,

a city is what we take with us.
What we keep.
The snapshot of a street.
The aerial view of skyscrapers
in traffic congested avenues
neglect a million stories.
Like clouds, millions of passersby
forever glance at their reflections
in glass mirrored windows.
The unexpected garden
always surprises
behind the mask
of wall, like a pupil
of labyrinthine dimensions
behind the dullness of a closed lid.
And one can then, always digress
away from the linear,
geometrical order mortared
upon the wilderness.
Beyond a maze
of offices and condos,
the sudden glimpse of teal waves
arouses the blood
to rush unabated
to breathe in the lake's raw throb
like a child running towards home's open door
or a lover to an unobstructed kiss.
As if God, or everything
were indeed inside the eye of a needle,
mesmerizing our gaze unto itself
in the guise of water and sky;
in the treasure of unkempt weedy patches
thriving their unstructured possibilities
in the secrecy of an unseen alley;
peering from the manic stare
of a homeless beggar.

The apple tree again,
offering forever fruits of paradise
from the confines of a manmade atrium
like a warm feathered sparrow;
a heart beating
from the unlatched door
of a cage of ribs.

Evolution

On the drives in my car
I have plucked every memory
from the roads of this town
as if my repetitive meanderings
could have shucked them
of all referents.

Everyone has come and gone.

Died, been replaced.
Giving the illusion of continuity
to these suburban streets.

But nothing is the same.

Strangeness has moved in
like a new neighbour.

It inhabits the old houses now.
Embodies the foliage of the old trees.
It has even settled into my own heart.

There are faces with new names
looking out of the renovated doors.

They are pale, holy hosts
exalting a short-lived sacredness
from gilded tabernacles.

Thrift shop

Once it was new.

Shone crisp on glam
Black plastic mannequins
In a signature boutique.

Ticketed with overpriced tag,
Exuded elusive utopias
Of ageless beauty. Style.

Now, it is here.

Jammed in endless
Rows of metal hangers
On endless racks
Of discarded garments.

Reduced below clearance
Value, it taunts
The hunter-gatherer
In me to unearth
Its hidden treasure.

A perfect gem.
Some remnant to be reclaimed
Of magic. Newness
Throbbing like a young heart
In a world of faded things

Magical woods

(inspired by a painting by Canadian artist Geri Puley)

you could get lost in this
small view of peace

white on white on golden white
light permeating into copper shadows

here too is the soul of things

resting in the hidden corners
of unobserved places
too small to mention

the uneventful stories of tiny shrub habitats

small like the chambers of your heart
where no one has been for years

like you alone in your corner of the world

where beauty has come and gone
slipped away unobtrusively
without fanfare or notice

your beauty, like your love
such small events
in the scheme of things

yet how deep the glow
of light on snow bared roots

frozen blooms, hardy thistles

covered in ice crystals

infinitesimal magnification
of a larger universal design

here too is everything
you say

as you observe god like
the grand beauty of this small detail

this microcosm of wonder

here too is your soul

A jar of fireflies

I will always remember
My mother on an August night
As if every other moment before
Or after had coalesced into one
Giant memory of her.
Crux of all maternal symbology,
Moon and stars leavening
In the indigo belly of summer.
A fecundity of fireflies fluttering invisible
Flurries of wings, glowed a soft, slow magic.
Caught glints of her earrings
Amidst black curls falling
Upon her Renoir-print
Green flowered dress.
In the growing shadows
She told me things. I listened.
Watched her every move.
As she watered geranium
And basil in brick-edged
Garden beds. Petals
Pungent of earth.
Scent galvanizing
Time and space. Proust-like.
Involuntary.
Etching the wonder of the two of us
As we stood in some primordial paradise
While all around, a universe of galactic stardust
Revolved. Enveloped us. And from the microcosm,
New like undiscovered dreams
Thousands of fireflies promised illusions
Of ageless never nevers.
She was my planet. I was her small moon.
Together in our little garden, snug as the snails

Safely at a distance from both birth and death,
For one eternal moment, we stood certain
Upon that soil of lettuces and pale petunias,
While far off the streets buzzed
With their cacophony of cars and voices.
Up close, behind the laurel leaves, a scarab
Tucked away its iridescent wing. And the fig tree
Curled a webbed leaf around its purple fruit.
My mother's shadow held me close too.
Like a hushing. A silent belonging to the earth.
To the blood that bore us, like everything
And everyone before and after.
The earth holding us up like a new crop
For a seemingly endless season.

Picking lilacs

(at St. Mary's Pioneer Cemetery)

In the cemeteries
The lilacs bloom.
By chance, in May
We found their fragrant, purple loot
Shading the forgotten stones. Their obelisks
Adorned with weathered cherubs, doves
Eternally poised for flight, riveted
Instead by Newtonian laws of physics
To the gravity of the mossy earth.
Mother called us delinquent
For entering a sacred place
To pick a few lilac branches.
Delinquent for grabbing
What little we could grasp
Of beauty, while we could.
Armfuls of sunlight
We gathered innocently
Thieving life,
Briefly,
On sacred ground.

Out of nothing

Why do I feel most at home
On a day like this?
When after a night of heavy rain
Light smudges morning
Onto the hard edges of things.
It makes me want to ponder
Mystical philosophies
Of inner and outer worlds.
Me absorbing nature within
The porous skin
Of my poetic soul.
The whole of sky fluting
Out of myself like an extension
Of my brain with its pale
Aura of clouds folding coils
Of meaning into the grooves
Of my own grey matter.
On this foggy morning
The chrome-yellow centre line
Painted on the wet asphalt
Unfurls networks of neuronal highways
Intersecting through old, familiar
Yet forever changing channels of memories.
Like my own closed fists
The trees are holding onto their buds
Tightly in this precarious weather
Reticent to yield their essence
As they wait for the benevolent warmth
Of the sun to relent their bloom
Willingly. Reveal their full dendritic growth
Spilling clusters of flowers
Their pastel hues finally softening
The angular harshness of concrete objects

With heavy snowfalls of petals.
On a morning like this
Everything is on the verge
Of becoming.
Behind the veil of fog
Everything exists at once, somewhere
In this landscape of the visible,
The unseen, the erased.
Bombs exploding out of sight,
Somewhere in the synapses
Are muffled by magnolias
Blooming pink like dopamine.
Tragedies too, recede
Beyond the sunny conflagrations
Of forsythia.
Out of the mist, the sense of things
Emerges like an arm with a sword
From a cold grey lake.
My own pale hand holding the metal
Wand, retrieved from a stony prison
Where, with the precise eye
Of a sculptor, I have learned to chisel
Catastrophes and chimeras
Into marble Gods.

Of love and writing

you cannot force the poem

it comes when it will
on butterfly wings of kismet

sails whole with wind
blowing along deep blue oceans
hide their reasoned intricacies
beneath reality's perfect skin

words too, they pull
mind, heart, senses
to shared images of worlds
we all have known

like the dark, green brush strokes
of weather bent pines
cutting against wisps of white
in cool, blue northern skies

the evenings spent casting lines
in ponds of golden sunsets

while longings took flight
in the cries of the night owl

no, you cannot force the poem

it comes when it will
in the softness of a lover's face

with lips of promise
it will lure you

to unknown labyrinths
where mind meets mind

where heart's door unlatches
to the blissful, dangerous rush
of limitless space

Rain

It has been raining all day. All night
The rain has polished the roads to black opal
Mirroring streamers of uneven neon
In the billowing reflections of dark stone rivers.
The rain is doing its pointillism
Scattering cold diamond globules
On the needled tips of tall pines,
Scouring the night like an old green jar.
The trees and their soggy shadows
Have become slippery squids,
Tentacles looming skyward.
Some of them blemished
With strings of malfunctioning lights
Unsightly and irksome like aphids.
Wet spider webs
Hanging between branches,
And telephone wires
Glisten.
Drip tedium
Onto the wasted moments
That gather momentum
In puddles.
In the cul de sacs
Of time and space,
Bending
Around street corners.
Their bright signs
Marking nothingness with names
Beneath tall lamp posts
That bow their heads
Like watchful sentinels of silence.
And it dawns on me

That maybe,
The whole world is a giant spider web
Thread upon thread, spun
Into pathways of meaning.
Creation meandering
For its own sake
With its inherent calculations.
A universe to dwell upon
To be caught in
And that within it,
I too am spinning
Filaments from my own wrists
Like blood
Like words
To grip tightly with at the edges
Of my abyss
Casting nets of ropes
To rest upon
To fall into, if necessary.
A safety net
Of sense and beauty
Sticky
Like a trap.

Life rounded up

one
plus one equals
the sum of its parts
two
sometimes drags
haloes
of remainders
points in time
dotting
the shreds
of loves, places
bits damned
to repeat
the glitches
of broken promises
with their infinite minutiae
impeding
clear calculations
delete
only the digits
beyond our side
of point zero
matter
here
now
one
plus one
somehow
add up

The harbour

(Inspired by Ron Eady's painting of Stelco's Steel Plant in Hamilton)

The animals have fled
This God forsaken place.
Run away for cover
Into the remaining hideouts
Of forests, oases.
Humans too
Have run back somewhere
To the safety of their houses.
Away from the deathly reminders
Of rusted steel. Paranoias
Of dystopian futures.
Cancerous premonitions.
Orange-red sunlight
Infuses a fetid blight
Into ozone empty
Turquoise skies.
Vitriolic
Caustic blue
Un-potable lakes
Once bearers of life,
Now mere cauldrons
Of industrial fluid.
The in and out cleanse
Of the city's saleable steel.

The surface of things

Oh, how I walk on the surface of things!
Skimming the glass of mirrors,
While brewing deep
Below murky depths
Invisible, chaos waits
To unravel me.

Seduced by the thrill of danger,
I glimpse below the sunlit patina
Of my reflection
Encircled by rippled light.

My soul luring to dive
Into the centrifugal centre
Of all things desired.

Is it not peace I seek?

Perhaps a new dimension.
Sequential regression
From ungraspable complexity
Into a simpler state
Of molecular suspension

In that mystical, foggy time
When atoms of my flesh
Had not collapsed
From waves to matter yet.

When no decisions had been made
In that unknown, forever time
When I did not exist.

Raison d'etre

this is the urgent poem

voice
giving
birth
to the child
heart
animal caged
escaping

human
without haloes
without wings

visceral, primal call
of death destined Eros
suddenly aware
of Eden's long told lie

mind's frantic computation
of the body's tawdry wrestle
with the world

Your return

The sound of your voice
makes the world
right again.

Stitches earth to sky.

All in order
as it should be.

Finally,
the moth-like, high rising
flight of seagulls
scatters glitter
within the vault of a rainbow.

Tiny white wings
dissolving past storms
into copper gilded blue.

A pot of gold.

Green meadow magic
of elfin fortune.
Love-luck,
your return.

The long awaited salve
to bind the ever rifting chasm
of my unbridgeable grief.

Summer evening

on the opalescent ripples
of the lake at dusk

geese are lining up
in haphazard formations

spelling cryptic meanings
like black messages in Arabic

the sky, drunk with summer
lifts a copper goblet
into the coming night
spilling sunset
onto the dark spine
of Toronto's skyline
like so much crumpled tinfoil

on the other side, darkness
emits intermittent lights
on and off red
through the heavy foliage
of trees nestled along the horseshoe

hiding the Gotham like squalor
of Hamilton's industrial harbour

better here alone
on the rocks
in this hidden, silent cove
better here
under this large white moon
healer of my sins
this communion wafer

holy moon
threading an uneven line
from space to me
across the water
like the white seagull
hopping ever closer
on the algae covered stones
at my feet
with its carnivorous beak
its flat, fish eye
calculating to strike
perhaps to oust me
as if it sensed
the corpse in me
like some quantum premonition

Glendella house

(a historical home in Bronte, moved in order to build a condo)

a white star
painted on a window pane
is what remains
of Bill Hill's dream

a poem
of lake and sky

phlox
wild violet hues

tenacious beauty
reaffirming life's essence
upon the rubble
of a broken wall

such strange symbiosis
this gentling of nature upon history

but soon, a new, sturdy structure
will replace the chaos
of another era

the white star will shatter
under the blows
of a metal crane

and the pale blue shingles
of Glendella house
will vanish like ghosts
in Bronte's mists

the flowers too
will be upturned

purple blooms crowning rubble
replaced by clean, neat turf

Contemplation on a miniature jade fountain in a chinese restaurant

I can understand it now
the unknowing
of the endless waiting
in all the waiting places
of my life
with their dead end paradoxes
the whole picture of the forest
with all its trees intact
in a miniature, marble Chinese fountain
sitting on the front counter
of Tasty Yu's
capturing my gaze
as I wait for almond rice
with side sauce of sweet and sour,
fortune cookies
with paper strips of ancient wisdom
inserted inside like tiny blessings
a tiny replica of the world
perfectly revolving sphere
of waterfalls gently splashing
over hidden jade dragons
coiled around white mountains
poised to exhale their angry fire
at any moment
beneath the indifferent glare
of an orange stone sun
forever turning
onto the greenery of finely chiseled pines

the comforting refuge of grey pagodas
shoddily painted by underpaid artisans
the whole world
held in the metaphor
of one multicoloured ornament
of sun, nature, dragons
perpetrating their beautiful violence
onto the serendipitous cascade
of water, the peace of peasants
and animals surviving in their shelters

and as I leave with my order
the fish tank mural scene
papered in the exit hall
reiterates the mantra
with its incongruous giant gold fish
swimming aimlessly in grey waters
amidst faded turquoise reeds
the whole thing punctuated
by creases and bumps
of badly plastered walls, dirt
waxed into the corners
of worn out vinyl tiles
my own life splayed out
before my very eyes
like a Rorschach ink blot test

Immigrants fishing on the oakville pier

(Winner of Arborealis Anthology Contest)

Tonight, cold wind stitches the waves.
Gathers them up like crepe satin.
Threads flickers of light
Into their dark, jade depths.

Across the lake, white sails
Bite the sky's pale lip.
A regatta of shark teeth
Aimed at the unsuspecting neck of night.

A few men are fishing on the pier.
Beyond the shimmering sound of chimes
I can hear the echo of their foreign tongues.

Their silhouettes etch strange shadows
In the deepening blue of evening.
Weave smoke signals to the constellations
With their cigarettes' burning glitter
That will fall like ashen skin at their feet
As they sit and wait with lines and nets
For a mythic catch that may not come.

The stars cannot birth the words.
The fish they hook will not speak
The language of their soul's longing.

Beside them, the lighthouse
Painted red like a woman's mouth
Drags its long white tip.

Exhales pulsating light into the night.
Beguiles with her trance of promise.

But there are no words tonight.

Silence spills from the bloody heart
Of this metal, painted whore
As she gives and gives in the dark
Forever pretending to rescue
The lost and the drowning.

Murdered gods

they come back

repeat like the call of a drum
those moments that marked my time

like murdered Gods
in white shrouds of history

always there
waiting to be resurrected
behind the heavy stone
of reason's portals

corpses like Jesus, like holy ghosts
my divine trinities

me in love at twenty one
with you forever
telling me that I'm beautiful

nonna waving goodbye
at her door for the last time

my father's final words
from a hospital room stretcher
bloodied with the urgency
of a ruptured heart
a broken dream

my family on an emigrant ship:
four demoted kings and queens
bereft of crowns and constellations

a ship's glass door lifting up
like the globe of a compass
revealing the direction of death's alternative
a ladder and rescue boat below
wavering needles in the darkest centre of the Atlantic

a country left behind
a bluer sky
a mother tongue, a civilization

piazzas like the dark pupils of familiar eyes
their hazel streets at dusk, the strands of an iris
golden around the lens of things
black centre points of all future cohesion
from which everything else would spawn
from the tiniest remembered things
like atoms of the long gone
dust of all that matters

Love's treasure

This night is a pirate
With its scarf of stars.

Its earring moon.

Blue ink seagulls tattooed
On the flexing arm of an Indian sky.

Dreams take sail on milky blue seas
With the white shirt frills of curling waves
Spilling their lacy foam on belts of sand
On the washed out grey of old driftwood stumps.

Tonight a creaking ghost ship sails.
Love is the captain.
A pirate hidden behind the open canvas.

By the lighthouse
Beyond the fog,
A maiden waits.

Yes, and there is treasure too
In dusty trunks
Of ancient maps marked with crosses.
Worms burrowing in the empty eye sockets
Of yellowed skulls.
Hooks instead of hands.
Half burned candles.
Empty bottles of rum.
And so the story goes
Of a maiden, a pirate,
A carved out heart

Doomed to haunt the waves
Searching for missed treasure.

Lovers and stars
Like buried coins
In the chest of night.

Dangerous reflection

I am the ghost of a dove.

Invisible trembling of wind
Through the branches of trees
Bare in the throes of winter.

Did you hear the sudden thud
At your window pane?

Did you see me hit?
Did you look away?

It was so unexpected
This falling.

Having mistaken sky
In the solid reflection
Of your soul exposed
Like sun and clouds

Behind a cold, glass eye.

Emerald city

(shortlisted for the Malahat Review Open Season Award in 2014)

Rebuilding the crumbling walls
Of a ruined Golden Age
Should be no quest for a child, nostalgic
For home. Kansas, beyond the vortex
Of windstorm, beast and witch
Dismembering the ideal with wily artifice;
Lulling a girl's resolve in poppy fields,
To awaken, finally wizened in a Quadling Kingdom
Dusting off the slumber from her limbs
To resume step after eager step
Along a winding road of yellow
Brick, strategically placed like crumbs
Leading her back like familiar words
To maps of return voyages, scrolls
Of merit from the wise, in glass towers up ahead.
Surely, her wide-eyed awe, her peasant braids,
Her blue gingham pinafore may have been construed
For bumpkin gullibility. "And should I, at your harmless
innocence
Melt as I do?" Said the witch. * Arm in arm with an inconstant
Courage, an underrated brain and a gutbucket heart
Dorothy tore back the sash on a sham wizard.
"Click! Click!" Went the shoes. "Home!" Cried the heart.
"Just follow the road!" Said the brain. Her own words blinking
Like sunlit glass in her hands.
Like emeralds.
Keys to kingdoms.

(quote from Milton's* Paradise Lost, Book 4*)*

A lesson of pieces

I always thought
you had to be skewed
to love the broken
somberness of faces
Picasso painted.
Their surreal jutting
of eyes, out
in the periphery
of cheekbones, ear lobes
cut off in other hemispheres
of angular skin, marooned
in oceans of grey blue
backgrounds boldly etched
with charcoal darkness
while anemone hands throbbed
pink blooms out of proportion.

Life has taught me different.

I was wrong.

It was me who was skewed.
Blind to life's unraveling.
Psyche's anachronisms.
My soul a dormant pupa
too young to understand cubism.

It has been a slow learning
this lesson of pieces
of the seemingly stable
trust of terra firma
brewing at its molten core.
The skin of things tearing

at the seams, rearranging
previously held visions
into new configurations.
Life offering the same old
hypnotic illusions
of eternity in the guise
of forever new blooms
while behind them
the old ones fray.
Regroup, like the faces
in Pablo's paintings.
Wrinkle and break misshapen.
Morbid shadows
of their former selves.

Life's true desecration
of symmetry. Beauty
rearranged. Death, macabre
painting the final stroke.

Christmas memories

winter of tangerines and chestnuts
berries in holly boughs
when laughter rings in the cold night
like a million mini lights
and champagne glasses bubble
over with good wishes and cheer

it is then that I remember
past the stack of all the years
a kitchen of long ago

three women with white aprons
scrubbed hands readying whisks
and copper bowls, almonds,
lemons and olive oil
whipping egg whites and sugar
into mounds of snow

nonna, mamma and me
baking cookies for Christmas
biscotti, amaretti, meringues
sugar dolls with silver eyes
and red candied lips
my dolls to keep
nonna's tradition
passed down to her
from ancient times
like all her golden heirlooms

I was special to you, nonna
you, who saw in me, my self
you who loved the essence of me

you were a connoisseur of essences
almond, crème de cacao, anisette
your home made liqueurs in fancy bottles
spilling from tiny crystal glasses on silver trays

your crème de menthe spills
down from the green neon of stoplights now
onto wet roads on rainy nights
green like your crème de menthe
to soothe me, like your love
beyond the arms of space and time

I would get lost in your embrace, nonna
the grand-daughter in whom you saw yourself
your mother's face, maybe
the child who carries your name
and your cheekbones
into the future

Creation

Out of nothing
I have created love
silver webs of light
in endless days

memories
shining bright in photographs
of my children's play on sunny beaches
old willow trees turned pirate ship
fishing on Bronte Pier

it breaks me up
to reminisce
my children
their young voices
calling me in videos
now that they're men
now that they push me away
in search of masculine autonomy
I understand
I know it's right
and yet

I long for their cherub faces
sleepy after a bath
in soft flannel pyjamas
begging for one more bedtime story

it chokes me up
this lack of them
the way they used to be
this time passing
trampling on our sand castles

blowing out
yet another birthday cake of candles
another year
into a strange tomorrow

The aloe plant on my mother's windowsill

There's an aloe plant in my mother's kitchen.
Tender, botanical tentacles of lush, green, healing substance
reminiscent of ominous, exotic sea creatures.

It has sat there forever
in an old, glazed, clay pot from the seventies
beside a scratched, orange tea kettle.

How long has it been since my father died?
How many times did the morning coffee percolate
with the ebullient promise of a new day
when in the evening, my mother cried herself to sleep?
Alone, she washed the yellow linoleum.
She clung to her chores for comfort
clipping clothes pins from her lips to a blue laundry line
with damp, reddened fingers on crisply bleached, white sheets
blowing in the north wind of a thousand Canadian mornings.
My mother, safe in the small house my father bought for her
never wandering too far away from what held her there
to the repetitive breath of the commonplace.

Memories and time elapse in the hum of her old kitchen fan.

My mother's eyes are deep, dark pools, evocative of night.
What was it that I could never comprehend in them?
What meanings was she able to gather in the mauve blush of
her garden?
How many dreams did she fold and refold
in the meandering chocolate swirls of her Spanish sponge
cake?

My mother's aloe plant stands between her eyes and the
  majestic night.
Like everything else in her world, it is both tender and
  frightening.
It has faced the dark for so long,
it has learned to extrapolate light from the colour black.
It has remade itself in a new land.
Soft, yet tenacious creature.
Fragile flower, in the guise of a north star.

Summer dreams

Oakville pier
disappears in fog
on hot, muggy mornings

lake and sky blending in grey mist

on the wharf, the lighthouse
beckons the eye

red stripe on white

beyond mounds of wild grass
blue chicory
silver lace

along the Sixteenth Mile's murky waters
sailboats' tall masts sway
hypnotic

"Scarab," "Dreamin'," "Ulysses"

names for adventure
hulls to sail away on
at high seas

away from torpid waters
into blue oceans
new worlds
the sun

Driving home from toronto on the QEW

what can you write
about polluted sky

purple dusk corrupted
by gaseous heat wave,
while a tired moon
slices thick smog
with mellow light
smudging melancholy
on another loveless evening

what can you say
of highway madness

bumper to bumper rush
of red tail lights
mechanical passion
simulated joy
of car stereo love songs
filling in the void
that grows
between our seat belted bodies
like air

Saturday night in suburbia

another Saturday night
swallows the remains of the day
choking on the fading light
of a deluded promise

drawn by the lure of neon signs
our car headlights glare
exhuming shadows silhouetted
against darkening trees and rooftops

another Saturday night in suburbia
buying hope at Seven-Eleven
popcorn, coke, movies

we will scratch off this night too
like all the others before
like numbers on a lottery ticket
anticipating to win
yet always losing

our hearts primed
to cash in on "big love"
settling fort snacks and entertainment

War on the planet

At this very moment
someone is dying.

Another Christ
is staggering in a city alley
or behind a barbed wire wall,
in a desert
to his own Golgotha,
that ever present place of skulls.

Random is this death.
Multiplied to the 'nth power of blood
under the light of a relentless sun.

At this very moment
a child is being born.
Bundles of hope
swaddled in innocence, while
with their strategic plans and war scrolls,
corporations and heads of state
wait to harvest him away
from his crib of dreams and lullabies.

At this very moment
a poet is writing
of men dying,
of children hatching in mine fields,
while scornful
the powerful plot their ploys of gain
unaffected by poems or human tears.

Moonless dark

this is a night of storms
the kind that swells evening waves
surprising us with moonless dark

rain splintering against window panes
reopening old wounds

this is a night of storms
rage of high winds
tormented sleep
howling lake and trees
dragging torrents of memories
into gutters, merging reality
with dreams, nightmares

fear's cold hands on my shoulders
lightning crackling at the window

this house or another
love here, or gone

Broken glass

Where do illusions go when they shatter?

I have seen shards of them glistening
on the rising crest of waves. Flickering
in the shivering sheen of trees
blowing helplessly in autumn wind.

Where do broken dreams go when they fall?

They come down from our eyes
clearing our view of the world with tears
like terse, grey skies after a heavy rain.

I have seen illusions run like dead November leaves
in the enthusiastic footsteps of children.

Sparks of them glowing in the flames
of stained glass summer lanterns.

Illusions go. We finally let go
of them like dead loved ones,
releasing their ashes to water and wind
in the relentless doing and undoing of the world.

Victoria day fireworks

it is breathtaking
this love

sparking in blue dusk
like fireworks

blasting off
in my heart
with the illusory excitement
of artificial star dust

thundering
with diamond explosions
in the cool night

love falling
like stars
in dark lakes
of loneliness

I could keep it forever
a love like this

sparklers weaving excitement
in the dark
with promises of summer
on the exulted cusp of spring

may it never fizzle out
this love

may it re-ignite forever
like galaxies in black space

to light our way
like bits of heaven

stepping stones
for our lost, lonely selves

Trajectory

I like telephone poles

there's a row of them in my backyard

black wires disappearing in tall pines
along some imaginary trajectory
back in time...

... sunlight breaks on the sea's horizon

... large, golden waves roll in from the Adriatic
along stretches of sandy beaches
speckled with colourful umbrellas

... a train speeds out of a black mountain tunnel
weaving through endless rows of poplars
around the blonde hills of wheat and oleander
below towns of church towers and terracotta rooftops
appearing and disappearing in sunlight...

these are the stitched up photographs
of a country I carry in my soul

Mediterranean blue skies
transcending time and space

when I look out the window
telephone poles always lead me back
along the wires...

... back to the first encounter with the ocean
to the hometown in my heart

when I was young and the world
was raw sensation
like the first impact with Eden

back when time was a thing of joy
and every fruit was mine for the taking

My human identity

I am a social construct.
Word upon word like blood.
Image upon image like flesh.

A technicolor film
of places and stories
I have lived through.

I am walking, breathing memory.
Frame by frame repository
of history's collective thoughts
in my seemingly separate cranium.

I walk this earth for a slice of time
oxidizing change with my cellular breath.

I am a biological reaction.
An evolutionary specimen of higher order thinking
passing on my essence to future gametes.
New versions of me
projecting holograms into the future.

I am a social construct.
I belong where memory shapes me.
In that space where I have put my feet down
to create meaning.

A poem from my laundry room

Cloistered beneath the surface
The world is strangely safe
As if a cave could quell
My urge to hope for wings.

The sky's vastness is but a patch
Of distant blue. The world
One branch of spruce, framed
In a basement window pane.

Down here, my soul
Stands still in the unpretentious
Slippers of my mother role.
Resists in that rush of life, bubbling;
Spilling like lemon scented suds
In grey enamel laundry tubs.

The hampers are filled
With yesterday's garments.
Those desiccated skins we have shed
Like faded memories of our lost selves,
While we wait for redemption
In the ritual of another day of cleansing.

Here are tidy boxes of new, improved soap,
Bleach bottles; segments of chaos neatly folded
Into piles of cotton and terrycloth;
Aluminum pipes, the arms of a furnace;
Wilderness branching out from the heart,
At the centre of this house; my self.

Down here I have imagined
Fresh starts, strangely grounded

In the vortex of a spin cycle; wrung out
Many illusions, ironing creases
From the years, while love songs
Played on an old radio.

From my small basement window
The world is one black patch
Of night; one snow covered branch
Of spruce; one moonlit cloud
Framed in one pane; one star.

Fall in our town

fall comes back on our town
blowing crisp wind
on the sunny, yellow morning of leaves
blushing like golden apples against crystal blue
skies, and it's the same beauties
accruing onto our paths
the same old dreams we rake
the same ancient maples re-enacting their splendour
in the vestiges of another season
life showing off the best of itself
in the hues of sun and blood
before bowing for the last time
again, on the stage of the world

Weathervane

Above the rooftop cupola you point north
Then east and west, or south again repeatedly.

Sideswiped by wind, the driver of the wagon steers
his horses through unpredictable fronts. Steadfast

the metal arrow soldered through the pivot
of both carriage and man, gives reliable direction
while obliging to eternal theorems of mass times velocity.

No love or choice, but physics rotates you, my rooftop
decoration.

A metal cowboy in a metal wagon, in metal hat and scarf.

Metal horses in perennial gallop and in front of them
a metal pointing compass, static on muggy days. Stuck

in some past point in time, like a clock hand stopped
at some bygone hour, its wheels in need of winding.

Where will you lead me today weather vane?

Did you notice the missing tile in the cupola that holds you
up?

Did you see the roof shingles curling up in sun parched
disarray?

In your unremitting pointing, did you notice the neighbours
moving, dying, losing their mind? Their houses being gutted?

Did you notice the new villa replacing the yellow siding house?
Where were you when it all happened, weathervane?

In your steel solidity you lead everyone to the tune of wind
Iconic western black artifact of a bygone era.
Soon, they will take you too. Dismantle your centre point
and unhinge you from the crux of your seemingly strong tower
while everything will fold beneath your conestoga wheels.
For a little longer, until then, you will lead us, finite like human thoughts,
to infinite certainties. You will reign through a few more handfuls of summer nights
in search of north stars; reign firm through a few more killer winter storms.
If you're lucky to avoid the fate of disappearing in a builder's dumpster,
you will keep on pointing as a memento on someone's wall or shelf;
pointing north towards some dream
galvanized on your image by your maker, of destinations
reachable through your dispassionate advice,
through having aged so well through wind and sun;
your simple guiding arrow towards the absolute
while unrelenting, entropy will take you too and everything.

Elements

(a poem commissioned by Justine Giuliani for the opening ceremonies of the Burlington Labyrinth, which she funded as a memorial for the death of her teenaged daughter)

three uncarved stones
bid us welcome
before gothic garden gates
leading our longing souls
to oasis of mystical labyrinth

deep in the circle
silence caresses our brow
redeeming brokenness

beneath benevolent evergreens
gentle paths of prayer beckon

peace, love, nature
the universe within
elements without

breath after footstep
heartbeat in sync
with the rhythm of earth and air

at the entrance of ourselves
a trinity of uncarved stones
stands, unveiling mystery

sparkling like a million diamonds
in the celebration of sunlight

look at the stones
and find your own stars
your own angels
before the gates of heaven

"come into the labyrinth!" they sing
"enter eternity within your own heart!"

www.ingramcontent.com/pod-product-compliance
Ingram Content Group UK Ltd.
Pitfield, Milton Keynes, MK11 3LW, UK
UKHW020422250726
13967UKWH00007B/2776